CW00495632

# RICH

Meeting the Loving Father

## St John Paul II

*All booklets are published thanks to the
generous support of the members of the
Catholic Truth Society*

CATHOLIC TRUTH SOCIETY
PUBLISHERS TO THE HOLY SEE

# Contents

*First published 2016 by the Incorporated Catholic Truth Society, 40-46*
*Harleyford Road, London SE11 5AY Tel: 020 7640 0042 Fax: 020 7640*
*7640 0046. Copyright © 2016 Libreria Editrice Vaticana, Citta del*
*Vaticano. This edition © 2016 The Incorporated Catholic Truth Society.*

*ISBN 978 178469 108 0*

# HE WHO SEES ME
# SEES THE FATHER

(cf. John 14:9)

### The revelation of mercy

It is "God, who is rich in mercy"[1] whom Jesus Christ has revealed to us as Father: it is His very Son who, in Himself, has manifested Him and made Him known to us.[2] Memorable in this regard is the moment when Philip, one of the twelve Apostles, turned to Christ and said: "Lord, show us the Father, and we shall be satisfied"; and Jesus replied: "Have I been with you so long, and yet you do not know me…? He who has seen me has seen the Father."[3] These words were spoken during the farewell discourse at the end of the paschal supper, which was followed by the events of those holy days during which confirmation was to be given once and for all of the fact that "God, who is rich in mercy, out of the great love with which he loved us, even when we were dead through our trespasses, made us alive together with Christ."[4]

Following the teaching of the Second Vatican Council and paying close attention to the special needs of our times, I devoted the encyclical *Redemptor hominis* to the truth about man, a truth that is revealed to us in its fullness and depth in Christ. A no less important need in these critical and difficult times impels me to draw attention once again in Christ to the countenance of the "Father of mercies and God of all comfort."[5] We read in the Constitution *Gaudium et spes*: "Christ the new Adam…fully reveals man to himself and brings to light his lofty calling," and does it "in the very revelation of the mystery of the Father and of his love."[6] The words that I have quoted are clear testimony to the fact that man cannot be manifested in the full dignity of his nature without reference - not only on the level of concepts but also in an integrally existential way - to God. Man and man's lofty calling are revealed in Christ through the revelation of the mystery of the Father and His love.

For this reason it is now fitting to reflect on this mystery. It is called for by the varied experiences of the Church and of contemporary man. It is also demanded by the pleas of many human hearts, their sufferings and hopes, their anxieties and expectations. While it is true that every individual human being is, as I said in my encyclical *Redemptor hominis*, the way for the Church, at the same time the Gospel and the whole of Tradition constantly show us that we must travel this day with every individual just as Christ traced it out by revealing in Himself the Father and His love.[7] In Jesus Christ, every path to man, as it has been assigned once and for all to the Church in the changing context of the times, is simultaneously an approach to the Father and His love. The Second Vatican Council has confirmed this truth for our time.

The more the Church's mission is centred upon man - the more it is, so to speak, anthropocentric - the more it must be confirmed and actualised theocentrically, that is to say, be directed in Jesus Christ to the Father. While the various currents of human thought both in the past and at the present have tended and still tend to separate theocentrism and anthropocentrism, and even to set them in opposition to each other, the Church, following Christ, seeks to link them up in human history, in a deep and organic way. And this is also one of the basic principles, perhaps the most important one, of the teaching of the last Council. Since, therefore, in the present phase of the Church's history we put before ourselves as our primary task the implementation of the doctrine of the great Council, we must act upon this principle with faith, with an open mind and with all our heart. In the encyclical already referred to, I have tried to show that the deepening and the many-faceted enrichment of the Church's consciousness resulting from the Council must open our minds and our hearts more widely to Christ. Today I wish to say that openness to Christ, who as the Redeemer of the world fully reveals man himself," can only be achieved through an ever more mature reference to the Father and His love.

## The incarnation of mercy

Although God "dwells in unapproachable light,"[8] He speaks to man by means of the whole of the universe: "ever since the creation of the world his invisible nature, namely, his eternal power and deity, has been clearly perceived in the things that have been made."[9] This indirect and imperfect knowledge, achieved by the intellect seeking God by means of creatures through the visible world, falls short of "vision of the Father." "No one has ever seen God," writes St John, in order to stress the truth that "the only Son, who is in the bosom of the Father, he has made him known."[10] This "making known" reveals God in the most profound mystery of His being, one and three, surrounded by "unapproachable light."[11] Nevertheless, through this "making known" by Christ we know God above all in His relationship of love for man: in His "philanthropy."[12] It is precisely here that "His invisible nature" becomes in a special way "visible," incomparably more visible than through all the other "things that have been made": it becomes visible in Christ and through Christ, through His actions and His words, and finally through His death on the cross and His resurrection.

In this way, in Christ and through Christ, God also becomes especially visible in His mercy; that is to say, there is emphasised that attribute of the divinity which the Old Testament, using various concepts and terms, already defined as "mercy." Christ confers on the whole of the

Old Testament tradition about God's mercy a definitive meaning. Not only does He speak of it and explain it by the use of comparisons and parables, but above all He Himself makes it incarnate and personifies it. He Himself, in a certain sense, is mercy. To the person who sees it in Him - and finds it in Him - God becomes "visible" in a particular way as the Father who is rich in mercy."[13]

The present-day mentality, more perhaps than that of people in the past, seems opposed to a God of mercy, and in fact tends to exclude from life and to remove from the human heart the very idea of mercy. The word and the concept of "mercy" seem to cause uneasiness in man, who, thanks to the enormous development of science and technology, never before known in history, has become the master of the earth and has subdued and dominated it.[14] This dominion over the earth, sometimes understood in a one-sided and superficial way, seems to have no room for mercy. However, in this regard we can profitably refer to the picture of "man's situation in the world today" as described at the beginning of the Constitution *Gaudium et spes*. Here we read the following sentences: "In the light of the foregoing factors there appears the dichotomy of a world that is at once powerful and weak, capable of doing what is noble and what is base, disposed to freedom and slavery, progress and decline, brotherhood and hatred. Man is growing conscious that the forces he has unleashed are in his own hands and that it is up to him to control them or be enslaved by them."[15]

The situation of the world today not only displays transformations that give grounds for hope in a better future for man on earth, but also reveals a multitude of threats, far surpassing those known up till now. Without ceasing to point out these threats on various occasions (as in addresses at UNO, to UNESCO, to FAO and elsewhere), the Church must at the same time examine them in the light of the truth received from God.

The truth, revealed in Christ, about God the "Father of mercies,"[16] enables us to "see" Him as particularly close to man especially when man is suffering, when he is under threat at the very heart of his existence and dignity. And this is why, in the situation of the Church and the world today, many individuals and groups guided by a lively sense of faith are turning, I would say almost spontaneously, to the mercy of God. They are certainly being moved to do this by Christ Himself, who through His Spirit works within human hearts. For the mystery of God the "Father of mercies" revealed by Christ becomes, in the context of today's threats to man, as it were a unique appeal addressed to the Church.

In the present encyclical wish to accept this appeal; I wish to draw from the eternal and at the same time - for its simplicity and depth - incomparable language of revelation and faith, in order through this same language to express once more before God and before humanity the major anxieties of our time.

In fact, revelation and faith teach us not only to meditate in the abstract upon the mystery of God as "Father of mercies," but also to have recourse to that mercy in the name of Christ and in union with Him. Did not Christ say that our Father, who "sees in secret,"[17] is always waiting for us to have recourse to Him in every need and always waiting for us to study His mystery: the mystery of the Father and His love?[18]

I therefore wish these considerations to bring this mystery closer to everyone. At the same time I wish them to be a heartfelt appeal by the Church to mercy, which humanity and the modern world need so much. And they need mercy even though they often do not realise it.

# The Messianic Message

**When Christ began to act and to teach**

Before His own townspeople, in Nazareth, Christ refers to the words of the prophet Isaiah: "The Spirit of the Lord is upon me, because he has anointed me to preach good news to the poor. He has sent me to proclaim release to the captives and recovering of sight to the blind, to set at liberty those who are oppressed, to proclaim the acceptable year of the Lord."[19] These phrases, according to Luke, are His first messianic declaration. They are followed by the actions and words known through the Gospel. By these actions and words Christ makes the Father present among men. It is very significant that the people in question are especially the poor, those without means of subsistence, those deprived of their freedom, the blind who cannot see the beauty of creation, those living with broken hearts, or suffering from social injustice, and finally sinners. It is especially for these last that the Messiah becomes a particularly clear sign of God who is love, a sign of the Father. In this visible sign the people of our own time, just like the people then, can see the Father.

It is significant that, when the messengers sent by John the Baptist came to Jesus to ask Him: "Are you he who is to come, or shall we look for another?",[20] He answered by referring to the same testimony with which He had begun His teaching at Nazareth: "Go and tell John what it is that you have seen and heard: the blind receive their sight, the lame walk, lepers are cleansed, and the deaf hear, the dead are raised up, the poor have good news preached to them." He then ended with the words: "And blessed is he who takes no offense at me".[21]

Especially through His lifestyle and through His actions, Jesus revealed that love is present in the world in which we live - an effective love, a love that addresses itself to man and embraces everything that makes up his humanity. This love makes itself particularly noticed in contact with suffering, injustice and poverty - in contact with the whole historical "human condition," which in various ways manifests man's limitation and frailty, both physical and moral. It is precisely the mode and sphere in which love manifests itself that in biblical language is called "mercy."

Christ, then, reveals God who is Father, who is "love," as St John will express it in his first letter[22]; Christ reveals God as "rich in mercy," as we read in St Paul.[23] This truth is not just the subject of a teaching; it is a reality made present to us by Christ. Making the Father present as love and mercy is, in Christ's own consciousness, the fundamental touchstone of His mission as the Messiah; this is confirmed by the words that He uttered first in the synagogue at Nazareth and later in the presence of His disciples and of John the Baptist's messengers.

On the basis of this way of manifesting the presence of God who is Father, love and mercy, Jesus makes mercy one of the principal themes of His preaching. As is His custom, He first teaches "in parables," since these express better the very essence of things. It is sufficient to recall the parable of the prodigal son,[24] or the parable of the Good Samaritan,[25] but also - by contrast - the parable of the merciless servant.[26] There are many passages in the teaching of Christ that manifest love - mercy under some ever-fresh aspect. We need only consider the Good Shepherd who goes in search of the lost sheep,[27] or the woman who sweeps the house in search of the lost coin.[28] The Gospel writer who particularly treats of these themes in Christ's teaching is Luke, whose Gospel has earned the title of "the Gospel of mercy."

When one speaks of preaching, one encounters a problem of major importance with reference to the meaning of terms and the content of concepts, especially the content of the concept of "mercy" (in relationship to the concept of "love"). A grasp of the content of these concepts is the key to understanding the very reality of mercy. And this is what is most important for us. However, before devoting a further part of our considerations to this subject, that is to say, to establishing the meaning of the vocabulary and the content proper to the concept of mercy," we must note that Christ, in revealing the love - mercy of God, at the same time demanded from people that they also should be guided in their lives by love and mercy. This requirement forms part of the very essence of the messianic message, and constitutes the heart of the Gospel ethos. The Teacher expresses this both through the medium of the commandment which He describes as "the greatest,"[29] and also in the form of a blessing, when in the Sermon on the Mount He proclaims: "Blessed are the merciful, for they shall obtain mercy."[30]

In this way, the messianic message about mercy preserves a particular divine-human dimension. Christ - the very fulfillment of the messianic prophecy - by becoming the incarnation of the love that is manifested with particular force with regard to the suffering, the unfortunate and sinners, makes present and thus more fully reveals the Father, who is God "rich in mercy." At the same time, by becoming for people a model of merciful love for others, Christ proclaims by His actions even more than by His words that call to mercy which is one of the essential elements of the Gospel ethos. In this instance it is not just a case of fulfilling a commandment or an obligation of an ethical nature; it is also a case of satisfying a condition of major importance for God to reveal Himself in His mercy to man: "The merciful...shall obtain mercy."

# The Old Testament

## The concept of "mercy" in the Old Testament

The concept of "mercy" in the Old Testament has a long and rich history. We have to refer back to it in order that the mercy revealed by Christ may shine forth more clearly. By revealing that mercy both through His actions and through His teaching, Christ addressed Himself to people who not only knew the concept of mercy, but who also, as the People of God of the Old Covenant, had drawn from their age-long history a special experience of the mercy of God. This experience was social and communal, as well as individual and interior.

Israel was, in fact, the people of the covenant with God, a covenant that it broke many times. Whenever it became aware of its infidelity - and in the history of Israel there was no lack of prophets and others who awakened this awareness - it appealed to mercy. In this regard, the books of the Old Testament give us very many examples. Among the events and texts of greater importance one may recall: the beginning of the history of the Judges,[31] the prayer of Solomon at the inauguration of the Temple,[32] part of the prophetic work of Micah,[33] the consoling assurances given by Isaiah,[34] the cry of the Jews in exile,[35] and the renewal of the covenant after the return from exile.[36]

It is significant that in their preaching the prophets link mercy, which they often refer to because of the people's sins, with the incisive image of love on God's part. The Lord loves Israel with the love of a special choosing, much like the love of a spouse,[37] and for this reason He pardons its sins and even its infidelities and betrayals. When He finds repentance and true conversion, He brings His people back to grace.[38] In the preaching of the prophets, mercy signifies a special power of love, which prevails over the sin and infidelity of the chosen people.

In this broad "social" context, mercy appears as a correlative to the interior experience of individuals languishing in a state of guilt or enduring every kind of suffering and misfortune. Both physical evil and moral evil, namely sin, cause the sons and daughters of Israel to turn to the Lord and beseech His mercy. In this way David turns to Him, conscious of the seriousness of his guilt[39]; Job too, after his rebellion, turns to Him in his tremendous misfortune[40]; so also does Esther, knowing the mortal threat to her own people.[41] And we find still other examples in the books of the Old Testament.[42]

At the root of this many-sided conviction, which is both communal and personal, and which is demonstrated by the whole of the Old Testament down the centuries, is the basic experience of the chosen people at the Exodus: the Lord saw the affliction of His people reduced to slavery, heard their cry, knew their sufferings and decided to deliver them.[43] In this act of salvation by the Lord, the prophet perceived his love and compassion.[44] This is precisely the grounds upon which the people and each of its members based their certainty of the mercy of God, which can be invoked whenever tragedy strikes.

Added to this is the fact that sin too constitutes man's misery. The people of the Old Covenant experienced this misery from the time of the Exodus, when they set up the golden calf. The Lord Himself triumphed over this act of breaking the covenant when He solemnly declared to Moses that He was a "God merciful and gracious, slow to anger, and abounding in steadfast love and faithfulness."[45] It is in this central revelation that the chosen people, and each of its members, will find, every time that they have sinned, the strength and the motive for turning to the Lord to remind Him of what He had exactly revealed about Himself[46] and to beseech His forgiveness.

Thus, in deeds and in words, the Lord revealed His mercy from the very beginnings of the people which He chose for Himself; and, in the course of its history, this people continually entrusted itself, both when stricken with misfortune and when it became aware of its sin, to the God of mercies. All the subtleties of love become manifest in the Lord's mercy towards those who are His own: He is their Father,[47] for Israel is His firstborn son[48]; the Lord is also the bridegroom of her whose new name the prophet proclaims: Ruhamah, "Beloved" or "she has obtained pity."[49]

Even when the Lord is exasperated by the infidelity of His people and thinks of finishing with it, it is still His tenderness and generous love for those who are His own which overcomes His anger.[50] Thus it is easy to understand why the psalmists, when they desire to sing the highest praises of the Lord, break forth into hymns to the God of love, tenderness, mercy and fidelity.[51]

From all this it follows that mercy does not pertain only to the notion of God, but it is something that characterises the life of the whole people of Israel and each of its sons and daughters: mercy is the content of intimacy with their Lord, the content of their dialogue with Him. Under precisely this aspect, mercy is presented in the individual books of the Old Testament with a great richness of expression. It may be difficult to find in these books a purely theoretical answer to the question of what mercy is in itself. Nevertheless, the terminology that is used is in itself able to tell us much about this subject.[52]

The Old Testament proclaims the mercy of the Lord by the use of many terms with related meanings; they are differentiated by their particular content, but it could be said that they all converge from different directions on one single fundamental content, to express its surpassing richness and at the same time to bring it close to man under different aspects. The Old Testament encourages people suffering from misfortune, especially those weighed down by sin - as also the whole of Israel, which had entered into the covenant with God - to appeal for mercy, and enables them to count upon it: it reminds them of His mercy in times of failure and loss of trust. Subsequently, the Old Testament gives thanks and glory for mercy every time that mercy is made manifest in the life of the people or in the lives of individuals.

In this way, mercy is in a certain sense contrasted with God's justice, and in many cases is shown to be not only more powerful than that justice but also more profound. Even the Old Testament teaches that, although justice is an authentic virtue in man, and in God signifies transcendent perfection nevertheless love is "greater" than justice: greater in the sense that it is primary and fundamental. Love, so to speak, conditions justice and, in the final analysis, justice serves love. The primacy and superiority of love vis-a-vis justice - this is a mark of the whole of revelation - are revealed precisely through mercy. This seemed so obvious to the psalmists and prophets that the very term justice ended up by meaning the salvation accomplished by the Lord and His mercy.[53] Mercy differs from justice, but is not in opposition to it, if we admit in the history of man - as the Old Testament precisely does- the presence of God, who already as Creator has linked Himself to His creature with a particular love. Love, by its very nature, excludes hatred and ill-will towards the one to whom He once gave the gift of Himself: *Nihil odisti eorum quae fecisti*, "you hold nothing of what you have made in abhorrence."[54] These words indicate the profound basis of the relationship between justice and mercy in God, in His relations with man and the world. They tell us that we must seek the life-giving roots and intimate reasons for this relationship by going back to "the beginning," in the very mystery of creation. They foreshadow in the context of the Old Covenant the full revelation of God, who is "love."[55]

Connected with the mystery of creation is the mystery of the election, which in a special way shaped the history of the people whose spiritual father is Abraham by virtue of his faith. Nevertheless, through this people which journeys forward through the history both of the Old Covenant and of the New, that mystery of election refers to every man and woman, to the whole great human family. "I have loved you with an everlasting love, therefore I have continued my faithfulness to you."[56] "For the mountains may depart…my steadfast love shall not depart from you, and my covenant of peace shall not be removed."[57] This truth, once proclaimed to Israel, involves a perspective of the whole history of man, a perspective both temporal and eschatological.[58] Christ reveals the Father within the framework of the same perspective and on ground already prepared, as many pages of the Old Testament writings demonstrate. At the end of this revelation, on the night before He dies, He says to the apostle Philip these memorable words: "Have I been with you so long, and yet you do not know me…? He who has seen me has seen the Father."[59]

# THE PARABLE OF THE PRODIGAL SON

### An analogy

At the very beginning of the New Testament, two voices resound in St Luke's Gospel in unique harmony concerning the mercy of God, a harmony which forcefully echoes the whole Old Testament tradition. They express the semantic elements linked to the differentiated terminology of the ancient books. Mary, entering the house of Zechariah, magnifies the Lord with all her soul for "his mercy," which "from generation to generation" is bestowed on those who fear Him. A little later, as she recalls the election of Israel, she proclaims the mercy which He who has chosen her holds "in remembrance" from all time.[60] Afterwards, in the same house, when John the Baptist is born, his father Zechariah blesses the God of Israel and glorifies Him for performing the mercy promised to our fathers and for remembering His holy covenant.[61]

In the teaching of Christ Himself, this image inherited from the Old Testament becomes at the same time simpler and more profound. This is perhaps most evident in the parable of the prodigal son.[62] Although the word "mercy" does not appear, it nevertheless expresses the essence of the divine mercy in a particularly clear way. This is due not so much to the terminology, as in the Old Testament books, as to the analogy that enables us to understand more fully the very mystery of mercy, as a profound drama played out between the father's love and the prodigality and sin of the son.

That son, who receives from the father the portion of the inheritance that is due to him and leaves home to squander it in a far country "in loose living," in a certain sense is the man of every period, beginning with the one who was the first to lose the inheritance of grace and original justice. The analogy at this point is very wide-ranging. The parable indirectly touches upon every breach of the covenant of love, every loss of grace, every sin. In this analogy there is less emphasis than in the prophetic tradition on the unfaithfulness of the whole people of Israel, although the analogy of the prodigal son may extend to this also. "When he had spent everything," the son "began to be in need," especially as "a great famine arose in that country" to which he had gone after leaving his father's house. And in this situation "he would gladly have fed on" anything, even "the pods that the swine ate," the swine that he herded for "one of the citizens of that country." But even this was refused him.

The analogy turns clearly towards man's interior. The inheritance that the son had received from his father was a quantity of material goods, but more important than these goods was his dignity as a son in his father's house. The situation in which he found himself when he lost the material goods should have made him aware of the loss of that dignity. He had not thought about it previously, when he had asked his father to give him the part of the inheritance that was due to him, in order to go away. He seems not to be conscious of it even now, when he says to himself: "How many of my father's hired servants have bread enough and to spare, but I perish here with hunger." He measures himself by the standard of the goods that he has lost, that he no longer "possesses," while the hired servants of his father's house "possess" them. These words express above all his attitude to material goods; nevertheless under their surface is concealed the tragedy of lost dignity, the awareness of squandered sonship.

It is at this point that he makes the decision: "I will arise and go to my father, and I will say to him, 'Father, I have sinned against heaven and before you; I am no longer worthy to be called your son. Treat me as one of your hired servants.'"[63] These are words that reveal more deeply the essential problem. Through the complex material situation in which the prodigal son found himself because of his folly, because of sin, the sense of lost dignity had matured. When he decides to return to his father's house, to ask his father to be received - no longer by virtue of his right as a son, but as an employee - at first sight he seems to be acting by reason of the hunger and poverty that he had fallen into; this motive, however, is permeated by an awareness of a deeper loss: to be a hired servant in his own father's house is certainly a great humiliation and source of shame. Nevertheless, the prodigal son is ready to undergo that humiliation and shame. He realises that he no longer has any right except to be an employee in his father's house. His decision is taken in full consciousness of what he has deserved and of what he can still have a right to in accordance with the norms of justice. Precisely this reasoning demonstrates that, at the centre of the prodigal son's consciousness, the sense of lost dignity is emerging, the sense of that dignity that springs from the relationship of the son with the father. And it is with this decision that he sets out.

In the parable of the prodigal son, the term "justice" is not used even once; just as in the original text the term "mercy" is not used either. Nevertheless, the relationship between justice and love, that is manifested as mercy, is inscribed with great exactness in the content of the Gospel parable. It becomes more evident that love is transformed into mercy when it is necessary to go beyond the precise norm of justice - precise and often too narrow. The prodigal son, having wasted the property he received from his father, deserves - after his return - to earn his living by working in his father's house as a hired servant and possibly, little by little, to build up a certain provision of material goods, though perhaps never as much as the amount he had squandered. This would be demanded by the order of justice, especially as the son had not only squandered the part of the inheritance belonging to him but had also hurt and offended his father by his whole conduct. Since this conduct had in his own eyes deprived him of his dignity as a son, it could not be a matter of indifference to his father. It was bound to make him suffer. It was also bound to implicate him in some way. And yet, after all, it was his own son who was involved, and such a relationship could never be altered or destroyed by any sort of behaviour. The prodigal son is aware of this and it is precisely this awareness that shows him clearly the dignity which he has lost and which makes him honestly evaluate the position that he could still expect in his father's house.

## Particular concentration on human dignity

This exact picture of the prodigal son's state of mind enables us to understand exactly what the mercy of God consists in. There is no doubt that in this simple but penetrating analogy the figure of the father reveals to us God as Father. The conduct of the father in the parable and his whole behaviour, which manifests his internal attitude, enables us to rediscover the individual threads of the Old Testament vision of mercy in a synthesis which is totally new, full of simplicity and depth. The father of the prodigal son is faithful to his fatherhood, faithful to the love that he had always lavished on his son. This fidelity is expressed in the parable not only by his immediate readiness to welcome him home when he returns after having squandered his inheritance; it is expressed even more fully by that joy, that merrymaking for the squanderer after his return, merrymaking which is so generous that it provokes the opposition and hatred of the elder brother, who had never gone far away from his father and had never abandoned the home.

The father's fidelity to himself - a trait already known by the Old Testament term *hesed* - is at the same time expressed in a manner particularly charged with affection. We read, in fact, that when the father saw the prodigal son returning home "he had compassion, ran to meet him, threw his arms around his neck and kissed him."[64] He certainly does this under the influence of a deep affection, and this also explains his generosity towards his son, that generosity which so angers the elder son. Nevertheless, the causes of this emotion are to be sought at a deeper level. Notice, the father is aware that a fundamental good has been saved: the good of his son's humanity. Although the son has squandered the inheritance, nevertheless his humanity is saved. Indeed, it has been, in a way, found again. The father's words to the elder son reveal this: "It was fitting to make merry and be glad, for this your brother was dead and is alive; he was lost and is found."[65] In the same chapter fifteen of Luke's Gospel, we read the parable of the sheep that was found[66] and then the parable of the coin that was found.[67] Each time there is an emphasis on the same joy that is present in the case of the prodigal son. The father's fidelity to himself is totally concentrated upon the humanity of the lost son, upon his dignity. This explains above all his joyous emotion at the moment of the son's return home.

Going on, one can therefore say that the love for the son the love that springs from the very essence of fatherhood, in a way obliges the father to be concerned about his son's dignity. This concern is the measure of his love, the love of which Saint Paul was to write: "Love is patient and kind... love does not insist on its own way; it is not irritable or resentful... but rejoices in the right... hopes all things, endures all things" and "love never ends."[68] Mercy - as Christ has presented it in the parable of the prodigal son - has the interior form of the love that in the New Testament is called agape. This love is able to reach down to every prodigal son, to every human misery, and above all to every form of moral misery, to sin. When this happens, the person who is the object of mercy does not feel humiliated, but rather found again and "restored to value." The father first and foremost expresses to him his joy that he has been "found again" and that he has "returned to life. This joy indicates a good that has remained intact: even if he is a prodigal, a son does not cease to be truly his father's son; it also indicates a good that has been found again, which in the case of the prodigal son was his return to the truth about himself.

What took place in the relationship between the father and the son in Christ's parable is not to be evaluated "from the outside." Our prejudices about mercy are mostly the result of appraising them only from the outside. At times it happens that by following this method of evaluation we see in mercy above all a relationship of inequality between the one offering it and the one receiving it. And, in consequence, we are quick to deduce that mercy belittles the receiver, that it offends the dignity of man. The parable of the prodigal son shows that the reality is different: the relationship of mercy is based on the common experience of that good which is man, on the common experience of the dignity that is proper to him. This common experience makes the prodigal son begin to see himself and his actions in their full truth (this vision in truth is a genuine form of humility); on the other hand, for this very reason he becomes a particular good for his father: the father sees so clearly the good which has been achieved thanks to a mysterious radiation of truth and love, that he seems to forget all the evil which the son had committed.

The parable of the prodigal son expresses in a simple but profound way the reality of conversion. Conversion is the most concrete expression of the working of love and of the presence of mercy in the human world. The true and proper meaning of mercy does not consist only in looking, however penetratingly and compassionately, at moral, physical or material evil: mercy is manifested in its true and proper aspect when it restores to value, promotes and draws good from all the forms of evil existing in the world and in man. Understood in this way, mercy constitutes the fundamental content of the messianic message of Christ and the constitutive power of His mission. His disciples and followers understood and practised mercy in the same way. Mercy never ceased to reveal itself, in their hearts and in their actions, as an especially creative proof of the love which does not allow itself to be "conquered by evil," but overcomes "evil with good."[69] The genuine face of mercy has to be ever revealed anew. In spite of many prejudices, mercy seems particularly necessary for our times.

MISERICORDIA · I·N·R·I · SAPIENCIA

FIDES · SYNAGOGA

SPONSA · OBEDIENCIA

SOPHIA · GEREHARDVS COMES

# THE PASCHAL MYSTERY

**Mercy revealed in the cross and resurrection**

The messianic message of Christ and His activity among people end with the cross and resurrection. We have to penetrate deeply into this final event - which especially in the language of the Council is defined as the *Mysterium Paschale* - if we wish to express in depth the truth about mercy, as it has been revealed in depth in the history of our salvation. At this point of our considerations, we shall have to draw closer still to the content of the encyclical *Redemptor hominis*. If, in fact, the reality of the Redemption, in its human dimension, reveals the unheard-of greatness of man, *qui talem ac tantum meruit habere Redemptorem*,[70] at the same time the divine dimension of the redemption enables us, I would say, in the most empirical and "historical" way, to uncover the depth of that love which does not recoil before the extraordinary sacrifice of the Son, in order to satisfy the fidelity of the Creator and Father towards human beings, created in His image and chosen from "the beginning," in this Son, for grace and glory.

The events of Good Friday and, even before that, in prayer in Gethsemane, introduce a fundamental change into the whole course of the revelation of love and mercy in the messianic mission of Christ. The one who "went about doing good and healing"[71] and "curing every sickness and disease"[72] now Himself seems to merit the greatest mercy and to appeal for mercy, when He is arrested, abused, condemned, scourged, crowned with thorns, when He is nailed to the cross and dies amidst agonising torments.[73] It is then that He particularly deserves mercy from the people to whom He has done good, and He does not receive it. Even those who are closest to Him cannot protect Him and snatch Him from the hands of His oppressors. At this final stage of His messianic activity the words which the prophets, especially Isaiah, uttered concerning the Servant of Yahweh are fulfilled in Christ: "Through his stripes we are healed."[74]

Christ, as the man who suffers really and in a terrible way in the Garden of Olives and on Calvary, addresses Himself to the Father - that Father whose love He has preached to people, to whose mercy He has borne witness through all of His activity. But He is not spared - not even He - the terrible suffering of death on the cross: For our sake God made him to be sin who knew no sin,"[75] St Paul will write, summing up in a few words the whole depth of the cross and at the same time the divine dimension of the reality of the Redemption. Indeed this Redemption is the ultimate and definitive revelation of the holiness of God, who is the absolute fullness of perfection: fullness of justice and of love, since justice is based on love, flows from it and tends towards it. In the passion and death of Christ - in the fact that the Father did not spare His own Son, but "for our sake made him sin"[76] - absolute justice is expressed, for Christ undergoes the passion and cross because of the sins of humanity. This constitutes even a "superabundance" of justice, for the sins of man are "compensated for" by the sacrifice of the Man-God. Nevertheless, this justice, which is properly justice "to God's measure," springs completely from love: from the love of the Father and of the Son, and completely bears fruit in love. Precisely for this reason the divine justice revealed in the cross of Christ is "to God's measure," because it springs from love and is accomplished in love, producing fruits of salvation. The divine dimension of redemption is put into effect not only by bringing justice to bear upon sin, but also by restoring to love that creative power in man thanks also to which he once more has access to the fullness of life and holiness that come from God. In this way, redemption involves the revelation of mercy in its fullness.

The Paschal Mystery is the culmination of this revealing and effecting of mercy, which is able to justify man, to restore justice in the sense of that salvific order which God willed from the beginning in man and, through man, in the world. The suffering Christ speaks in a special way to man, and not only to the believer. The non-believer also will be able to discover in Him the eloquence of solidarity with the human lot, as also the harmonious fullness of a disinterested dedication to the cause of man, to truth and to love. And yet the divine dimension of the Paschal Mystery goes still deeper. The cross on Calvary, the cross upon which Christ conducts His final dialogue with the Father, emerges from the very heart of the love that man, created in the image and likeness of God, has been given as a gift, according to God's eternal plan. God, as Christ has revealed Him, does not merely remain closely linked with the world as the Creator and the ultimate source of existence. He is also Father: He is linked to man, whom He called to existence in the visible world, by a bond still more intimate than that of creation. It is love which not only creates the good but also grants participation in the very life of God: Father, Son and Holy Spirit. For he who loves desires to give himself.

The cross of Christ on Calvary stands beside the path of that admirable commercium, of that wonderful self-communication of God to man, which also includes the call to man to share in the divine life by giving himself, and with himself the whole visible world, to God, and like an adopted son to become a sharer in the truth and love which is in God and proceeds from God. It is precisely beside the path of man's eternal election to the dignity of being an adopted child of God that there stands in history the cross of Christ, the only-begotten Son, who, as "light from light, true God from true God,"[77] came to give the final witness to the wonderful covenant of God with humanity, of God with man - every human being. This covenant, as old as man - it goes back to the very mystery of creation - and afterwards many times renewed with one single chosen people, is equally the new and definitive covenant, which was established there on Calvary, and is not limited to a single people, to Israel, but is open to each and every individual.

What else, then, does the cross of Christ say to us, the cross that in a sense is the final word of His messianic message and mission? And yet this is not yet the word of the God of the covenant: that will be pronounced at the dawn when first the women and then the Apostles come to the tomb of the crucified Christ, see the tomb empty and for the first time hear the message: "He is risen." They will repeat this message to the others and will be witnesses to the risen Christ. Yet, even in this glorification of the Son of God, the cross remains, that cross which - through all the messianic testimony of the Man the Son, who suffered death upon it - speaks and never ceases to speak of God the Father, who is absolutely faithful to His eternal love for man, since He "so loved the world" - therefore man in the world - that "he gave his only Son, that whoever believes in him should not perish but have eternal life."[78] Believing in the crucified Son means "seeing the Father,"[79] means believing that love is present in the world and that this love is more powerful than any kind of evil in which individuals, humanity, or the world are involved. Believing in this love means believing in mercy. For mercy is an indispensable dimension of love; it is as it were love's second name and, at the same time, the specific manner in which love is revealed and effected vis-a-vis the reality of the evil that is in the world, affecting and besieging man, insinuating itself even into his heart and capable of causing him to "perish in Gehenna."[80]

### Love more powerful than death, more powerful than sin

The cross of Christ on Calvary is also a witness to the strength of evil against the very Son of God, against the one who, alone among all the sons of men, was by His nature absolutely innocent and free from sin, and whose coming into the world was untainted by the disobedience of Adam and the inheritance of original sin. And here, precisely in Him, in Christ, justice is done to sin at the price of His sacrifice, of His obedience "even to death."[81] He who was without sin, "God made him sin for our sake."[82] Justice is also brought to bear upon death, which from the beginning of man's history had been allied to sin. Death has justice done to it at the price of the death of the one who was without sin and who alone was able - by means of his own death - to inflict death upon death.[83] In this way the cross of Christ, on which the Son, consubstantial with the Father, renders full justice to God, is also a radical revelation of mercy, or rather of the love that goes against what constitutes the very root of evil in the history of man: against sin and death.

The cross is the most profound condescension of God to man and to what man - especially in difficult and painful moments - looks on as his unhappy destiny. The cross is like a touch of eternal love upon the most painful wounds of man's earthly existence; it is the total fulfillment of the messianic program that Christ once formulated in the synagogue at Nazareth[84] and then repeated to the messengers sent by John the Baptist.[85] According to the words once written in the prophecy of Isaiah,[86] this program consisted in the revelation of merciful love for the poor, the suffering and prisoners, for the blind, the oppressed and sinners. In the paschal mystery the limits of the many sided evil in which man becomes a sharer during his earthly existence are surpassed: the cross of Christ, in fact, makes us understand the deepest roots of evil, which are fixed in sin and death; thus the cross becomes an eschatological sign. Only in the eschatological fulfillment and definitive renewal of the world will love conquer, in all the elect, the deepest sources of evil, bringing as its fully mature fruit the kingdom of life and holiness and glorious immortality. The foundation of this eschatological fulfillment is already contained in the cross of Christ and in His death. The fact that Christ "was raised the third day"[87] constitutes the final sign of the messianic mission, a sign that perfects the entire revelation of merciful love in a world that is subject to evil. At the same time it constitutes the sign that foretells "a new heaven and a new earth,"[88] when God "will wipe away every tear from their eyes, there will be no more death, or mourning no crying, nor pain, for the former things have passed away."[89]

In the eschatological fulfillment mercy will be revealed as love, while in the temporal phase, in human history, which is at the same time the history of sin and death, love must be revealed above all as mercy and must also be actualised as mercy. Christ's messianic program, the program of mercy, becomes the program of His people, the program of the Church. At its very centre there is always the cross, for it is in the cross that the revelation of merciful love attains its culmination. Until "the former things pass away,"[90] the cross will remain the point of reference for other words too of the Revelation of John: "Behold, I stand at the door and knock; if anyone hears my voice and opens the door, I will come in and eat with him and he with me."[91] In a special way, God also reveals His mercy when He invites man to have "mercy" on His only Son, the crucified one.

Christ, precisely as the crucified one, is the Word that does not pass away,[92] and He is the one who stands at the door and knocks at the heart of every man,[93] without restricting his freedom, but instead seeking to draw from this very freedom love, which is not only an act of solidarity with the suffering Son of man, but also a kind of "mercy" shown by each one of us to the Son of the eternal Father. In the whole of this messianic program of Christ, in the whole revelation of mercy through the cross, could man's dignity be more highly respected and ennobled, for, in obtaining mercy, He is in a sense the one who at the same time "shows mercy"? In a word, is not this the position of Christ with regard to man when He says: "As you did it to one of the least of these…you did it to me"?[94] Do not the words of the Sermon on the Mount: "Blessed are the merciful, for they shall obtain mercy,"[95] constitute, in a certain sense, a synthesis of the whole of the Good News, of the whole of the "wonderful exchange" (admirable commercium) contained therein? This exchange is a law of the very plan of salvation, a law which is simple, strong and at the same time "easy." Demonstrating from the very start what the "human heart" is capable of ("to be merciful"), do not these words from the Sermon on the Mount reveal in the same perspective the deep mystery of God: that inscrutable unity of Father, Son and Holy Spirit, in which love, containing justice, sets in motion mercy, which in its turn reveals the perfection of justice?

The Paschal Mystery is Christ at the summit of the revelation of the inscrutable mystery of God. It is precisely then that the words pronounced in the Upper Room are

40

completely fulfilled: "He who has seen me has seen the Father."[96] In fact, Christ, whom the Father "did not spare"[97] for the sake of man and who in His passion and in the torment of the cross did not obtain human mercy, has revealed in His resurrection the fullness of the love that the Father has for Him and, in Him, for all people. "He is not God of the dead, but of the living."[98] In His resurrection Christ has revealed the God of merciful love, precisely because He accepted the cross as the way to the resurrection. And it is for this reason that - when we recall the cross of Christ, His passion and death - our faith and hope are centred on the Risen One: on that Christ who "on the evening of that day, the first day of the week, ...stood among them" in the upper Room, "where the disciples were, ...breathed on them, and said to them: 'Receive the Holy Spirit. If you forgive the sins of any, they are forgiven; if you retain the sins of any, they are retained.'"[99]

Here is the Son of God, who in His resurrection experienced in a radical way mercy shown to Himself, that is to say the love of the Father which is more powerful than death. And it is also the same Christ, the Son of God, who at the end of His messianic mission - and, in a certain sense, even beyond the end - reveals Himself as the inexhaustible source of mercy, of the same love that, in a subsequent perspective of the history of salvation in the Church, is to be everlastingly confirmed as more powerful than sin. The paschal Christ is the definitive incarnation of mercy, its living sign in salvation history and in eschatology. In the same spirit, the liturgy of Eastertide places on our lips the words of the Psalm: *Misericordias Domini in aeternum cantabo*.[100]

## Mother of mercy

These words of the Church at Easter re-echo in the fullness of their prophetic content the words that Mary uttered during her visit to Elizabeth, the wife of Zechariah: "His mercy is…from generation to generation."[101] At the very moment of the Incarnation, these words open up a new perspective of salvation history. After the resurrection of Christ, this perspective is new on both the historical and the eschatological level. From that time onwards there is a succession of new generations of individuals in the immense human family, in ever-increasing dimensions; there is also a succession of new generations of the People of God, marked with the Sign of the Cross and of the resurrection and "sealed"[102] with the sign of the Paschal Mystery of Christ, the absolute revelation of the mercy that Mary proclaimed on the threshold of her kinswoman's house: "His mercy is…from generation to generation."[103]

Mary is also the one who obtained mercy in a particular and exceptional way, as no other person has. At the same time, still in an exceptional way, she made possible with the sacrifice of her heart her own sharing in revealing God's mercy. This sacrifice is intimately linked with the cross of her Son, at the foot of which she was to stand on Calvary. Her sacrifice is a unique sharing in the revelation of mercy, that is, a sharing in the absolute fidelity of God to His own love, to the covenant that He willed from eternity and that He entered into in time with man, with the people, with humanity; it is a sharing in that revelation that was definitively fulfilled through the cross. No one has experienced, to the same degree as the Mother of the crucified One, the mystery of the cross, the overwhelming encounter of divine transcendent justice with love: that "kiss" given by mercy to justice.[104] No one has received into his heart, as much as Mary did, that mystery, that truly divine dimension of the redemption effected on Calvary by means of the death of the Son, together with the sacrifice of her maternal heart, together with her definitive "fiat."

Mary, then, is the one who has the deepest knowledge of the mystery of God's mercy. She knows its price, she knows how great it is. In this sense, we call her the Mother of mercy: our Lady of mercy, or Mother of divine mercy; in each one of these titles there is a deep theological meaning, for they express the special preparation of her soul, of her whole personality, so that she was able to perceive, through the complex events, first of Israel, then of every individual and of the whole of humanity, that mercy of which "from generation to generation"[105] people become sharers according to the eternal design of the most Holy Trinity.

The above titles which we attribute to the Mother of God speak of her principally, however, as the Mother of the crucified and risen One; as the One who, having obtained mercy in an exceptional way, in an equally exceptional way "merits" that mercy throughout her earthly life and, particularly, at the foot of the cross of her Son; and finally as the one who, through her hidden and at the same time incomparable sharing in the messianic mission of her Son, was called in a special way to bring close to people that love which He had come to reveal: the love that finds its most concrete expression vis-a-vis the suffering, the poor, those deprived of their own freedom, the blind, the oppressed and sinners, just as Christ spoke of them in the words of the prophecy of Isaiah, first in the synagogue at Nazareth[106] and then in response to the question of the messengers of John the Baptist.[107]

It was precisely this "merciful" love, which is manifested above all in contact with moral and physical evil, that the heart of her who was the Mother of the crucified and risen One shared in singularly and exceptionally - that Mary shared in. In her and through her, this love continues to be revealed in the history of the Church and of humanity. This revelation is especially fruitful because in the Mother of God it is based upon the unique tact of her maternal heart, on her particular sensitivity, on her particular fitness to reach all those who most easily accept the merciful love of a mother. This is one of the great life-giving mysteries of Christianity, a mystery intimately connected with the mystery of the Incarnation.

"The motherhood of Mary in the order of grace," as the Second Vatican Council explains, "lasts without interruption from the consent which she faithfully gave at the annunciation and which she sustained without hesitation under the cross, until the eternal fulfillment of all the elect. In fact, being assumed into heaven she has not laid aside this office of salvation but by her manifold intercession she continues to obtain for us the graces of eternal salvation. By her maternal charity, she takes care of the brethren of her Son who still journey on earth surrounded by dangers and difficulties, until they are led into their blessed home."[108]

# "MERCY... FROM GENERATION TO GENERATION"

## An image of our generation

We have every right to believe that our generation too was included in the words of the Mother of God when she glorified that mercy shared in "from generation to generation" by those who allow themselves to be guided by the fear of God. The words of Mary's Magnificat have a prophetic content that concerns not only the past of Israel but also the whole future of the People of God on earth. In fact, all of us now living on earth are the generation that is aware of the approach of the third millennium and that profoundly feels the change that is occurring in history.

The present generation knows that it is in a privileged position: progress provides it with countless possibilities that only a few decades ago were undreamed of. Man's creative activity, his intelligence and his work, have brought about profound changes both in the field of science and technology and in that of social and cultural life. Man has extended his power over nature and has acquired deeper knowledge of the laws of social behaviour. He has seen the obstacles and distances between individuals and nations dissolve or shrink through an increased sense of what is universal, through a clearer awareness of the unity of the human race, through the acceptance of mutual dependence in authentic solidarity, and through the desire and possibility of making contact with one's brothers and sisters beyond artificial geographical divisions and national or racial limits. Today's young people, especially, know that the progress of science and technology can produce not only new material goods but also a wider sharing in knowledge. The extraordinary progress made in the field of information and data processing, for instance, will increase man's creative capacity and provide access to the intellectual and cultural riches of other peoples. New communications techniques will encourage greater participation in events and a wider exchange of ideas. The achievements of biological, psychological and social science will help man to understand better the riches of his own being. It is true that too often this progress is still the privilege of the industrialised countries, but it cannot be denied that the prospect of enabling every people and every country to benefit from it has long ceased to be a mere utopia when there is a real political desire for it.

But side by side with all this, or rather as part of it, there are also the difficulties that appear whenever there is growth. There is unease and a sense of powerlessness regarding the profound response that man knows that he must give. The picture of the world today also contains shadows and imbalances that are not always merely superficial. The Pastoral Constitution *Gaudium et spes* of the Second Vatican Council is certainly not the only document that deals with the life of this generation, but it is a document of particular importance. "The dichotomy affecting the modern world," we read in it, "is, in fact, a symptom of a deeper dichotomy that is in man himself. He is the meeting point of many conflicting forces. In his condition as a created being he is subject to a thousand shortcomings, but feels untrammelled in his inclinations and destined for a higher form of life. Torn by a welter of anxieties he is compelled to choose between them and repudiate some among them. Worse still, feeble and sinful as he is, he often does the very thing he hates and does not do what he wants. And so he feels himself divided, and the result is a host of discords in social life."[109]

Towards the end of the introductory exposition we read: "…in the face of modern developments there is a growing body of men who are asking the most fundamental of all questions or are glimpsing them with a keener insight: What is man? What is the meaning of suffering, evil, death, which have not been eliminated by all this progress? What is the purpose of these achievements, purchased at so high a price?"[110]

In the span of the fifteen years since the end of the Second Vatican Council, has this picture of tensions and threats that mark our epoch become less disquieting? It seems not. On the contrary, the tensions and threats that in the Council document seem only to be outlined and not to manifest in depth all the dangers hidden within them have revealed themselves more clearly in the space of these years; they have in a different way confirmed that danger, and do not permit us to cherish the illusions of the past.

## Sources of uneasiness

Thus, in our world the feeling of being under threat is increasing. There is an increase of that existential fear connected especially, as I said in the encyclical *Redemptor hominis*, with the prospect of a conflict that in view of today's atomic stockpiles could mean the partial self-destruction of humanity. But the threat does not merely concern what human beings can do to human beings through the means provided by military technology; it also concerns many other dangers produced by a materialistic society which - in spite of "humanistic" declarations - accepts the primacy of things over persons. Contemporary man, therefore, fears that by the use of the means invented by this type of society, individuals and the environment, communities, societies and nations can fall victim to the abuse of power by other individuals, environments and societies. The history of our century offers many examples of this. In spite of all the declarations on the rights of man in his integral dimension, that is to say in his bodily and spiritual existence, we cannot say that these examples belong only to the past.

Man rightly fears falling victim to an oppression that will deprive him of his interior freedom, of the possibility of expressing the truth of which he is convinced, of the faith that he professes, of the ability to obey the voice of conscience that tells him the right path to follow. The technical means at the disposal of modern society conceal within themselves not only the possibility of self-destruction through military conflict, but also the possibility of a "peaceful" subjugation of individuals, of environments, of entire societies and of nations, that for one reason or another might prove inconvenient for those who possess the necessary means and are ready to use them without scruple. An instance is the continued existence of torture, systematically used by authority as a means of domination and political oppression and practised by subordinates with impunity.

Together with awareness of the biological threat, therefore, there is a growing awareness of yet another threat, even more destructive of what is essentially human, what is intimately bound up with the dignity of the person and his or her right to truth and freedom.

All this is happening against the background of the gigantic remorse caused by the fact that, side by side with wealthy and surfeited people and societies, living in plenty and ruled by consumerism and pleasure, the same human family contains individuals and groups that are suffering from hunger. There are babies dying of hunger under their mothers' eyes. In various parts of the world, in various socio-economic systems, there exist entire areas of poverty, shortage and underdevelopment. This fact is universally known. The state of inequality between individuals and between nations not only still exists; it is increasing. It still happens that side by side with those who are wealthy and living in plenty there exist those who are living in want, suffering misery and often actually dying of hunger; and their number reaches tens, even hundreds of millions. This is why moral uneasiness is destined to become even more acute. It is obvious that a fundamental defect, or rather a series of defects, indeed a defective machinery is at the root of contemporary economics and materialistic civilisation, which does not allow the human family to break free from such radically unjust situations.

This picture of today's world in which there is so much evil both physical and moral, so as to make of it a world entangled in contradictions and tensions, and at the same time full of threats to human freedom, conscience and religion - this picture explains the uneasiness felt by contemporary man. This uneasiness is experienced not only by those who are disadvantaged or oppressed, but also by those who possess the privileges of wealth, progress and power. And, although there is no lack of people trying to understand the causes of this uneasiness, or trying to react against it with the temporary means offered by technology, wealth or power, still in the very depth of the human spirit this uneasiness is stronger than all temporary means. This uneasiness concerns - as the analyses of the Second Vatican Council rightly pointed out - the fundamental problems of all human existence. It is linked with the very sense of man's existence in the world, and is an uneasiness for the future of man and all humanity; it demands decisive solutions, which now seem to be forcing themselves upon the human race.

## Is justice enough?

It is not difficult to see that in the modern world the sense of justice has been reawakening on a vast scale; and without doubt this emphasises that which goes against justice in relationships between individuals, social groups and "classes," between individual peoples and states, and finally between whole political systems, indeed between what are called "worlds." This deep and varied trend, at the basis of which the contemporary human conscience has placed justice, gives proof of the ethical character of the tensions and struggles pervading the world.

The Church shares with the people of our time this profound and ardent desire for a life which is just in every aspect, nor does she fail to examine the various aspects of the sort of justice that the life of people and society demands. This is confirmed by the field of Catholic social doctrine, greatly developed in the course of the last century. On the lines of this teaching proceed the education and formation of human consciences in the spirit of justice, and also individual undertakings, especially in the sphere of the apostolate of the laity, which are developing in precisely this spirit.

And yet, it would be difficult not to notice that very often programs which start from the idea of justice and which ought to assist its fulfillment among individuals, groups and human societies, in practice suffer from distortions. Although they continue to appeal to the idea of justice, nevertheless experience shows that other negative forces have gained the upper hand over justice, such as spite, hatred and even cruelty. In such cases, the desire to annihilate the enemy, limit his freedom, or even force him into total dependence, becomes the fundamental motive for action; and this contrasts with the essence of justice, which by its nature tends to establish equality and harmony between the parties in conflict. This kind of abuse of the idea of justice and the practical distortion of it show how far human action can deviate from justice itself, even when it is being undertaken in the name of justice. Not in vain did Christ challenge His listeners, faithful to the doctrine of the Old Testament, for their attitude which was manifested in the words: An eye for an eye and a tooth for a tooth."[111] This was the form of distortion of justice at that time; and today's forms continue to be modeled on it. It is obvious, in fact, that in the name of an alleged justice (for example, historical justice or class justice) the neighbour is sometimes destroyed, killed, deprived of liberty or stripped of fundamental human rights. The experience of the past and of our own time demonstrates that justice alone is not enough, that it can even lead to the negation and destruction of itself, if that deeper power, which is love, is not allowed to shape human life in its various dimensions. It has been precisely historical experience that, among other things, has led to the formulation of the saying: *summum ius, summa iniuria*. This statement does not detract from the value of justice and does not minimise the significance of the order that is based upon it; it only indicates, under another aspect, the need to draw from the powers of the spirit which condition the very order of justice, powers which are still more profound.

The Church, having before her eyes the picture of the generation to which we belong, shares the uneasiness of so many of the people of our time. Moreover, one cannot fail to be worried by the decline of many fundamental values, which constitute an unquestionable good not only for Christian morality but simply for human morality, for moral culture: these values include respect for human life from the moment of conception, respect for marriage in its indissoluble unity, and respect for the stability of the family. Moral permissiveness strikes especially at this most sensitive sphere of life and society. Hand in hand with this go the crisis of truth in human relationships, lack of responsibility for what one says, the purely utilitarian relationship between individual and individual, the loss of a sense of the authentic common good and the ease with which this good is alienated. Finally, there is the "desacralisation" that often turns into "dehumanisation": the individual and the society for whom nothing is "sacred" suffer moral decay, in spite of appearances.

# THE MERCY OF GOD IN THE MISSION OF THE CHURCH

In connection with this picture of our generation, a picture which cannot fail to cause profound anxiety, there come to mind once more those words which, by reason of the Incarnation of the Son of God, resounded in Mary's Magnificat, and which sing of "mercy from generation to generation." The Church of our time, constantly pondering the eloquence of these inspired words, and applying them to the sufferings of the great human family, must become more particularly and profoundly conscious of the need to bear witness in her whole mission to God's mercy, following in the footsteps of the tradition of the Old and the New Covenant, and above all of Jesus Christ Himself and His Apostles. The Church must bear witness to the mercy of God revealed in Christ, in the whole of His mission as Messiah, professing it in the first place as a salvific truth of faith and as necessary for a life in harmony with faith, and then seeking to introduce it and to make it incarnate in the lives both of her faithful and as far as possible in the lives of all people of good will. Finally, the Church - professing mercy and remaining always faithful to it - has the right and the duty to call upon the mercy of God, imploring it in the face of all the manifestations of physical and moral evil, before all the threats that cloud the whole horizon of the life of humanity today.

## The Church professes the mercy of God and proclaims it

The Church must profess and proclaim God's mercy in all its truth, as it has been handed down to us by revelation. We have sought, in the foregoing pages of the present document, to give at least an outline of this truth, which finds such rich expression in the whole of Sacred Scripture and in Sacred Tradition. In the daily life of the Church the truth about the mercy of God, expressed in the Bible, resounds as a perennial echo through the many readings of the Sacred Liturgy. The authentic sense of faith of the People of God perceives this truth, as is shown by various expressions of personal and community piety. It would of course be difficult to give a list or summary of them all, since most of them are vividly inscribed in the depths of people's hearts and minds. Some theologians affirm that mercy is the greatest of the attributes and perfections of God, and the Bible, Tradition and the whole faith life of the People of God provide particular proofs of this. It is not a question here of the perfection of the inscrutable essence of God in the mystery of the divinity itself, but of the perfection and attribute whereby man, in the intimate truth of his existence, encounters the living God particularly closely and particularly often. In harmony with Christ's words to Philip,[112] the "vision of the Father" - a vision of God through faith finds precisely in the encounter with His mercy a unique moment of interior simplicity and truth, similar to that which we discover in the parable of the prodigal son.

"He who has seen me has seen the Father."[113] The Church professes the mercy of God, the Church lives by it in her wide experience of faith and also in her teaching, constantly contemplating Christ, concentrating on Him, on His life and on His Gospel, on His cross and resurrection, on His whole mystery. Everything that forms the "vision" of Christ in the Church's living faith and teaching brings us nearer to the "vision of the Father" in the holiness of His mercy. The Church seems in a particular way to profess the mercy of God and to venerate it when she directs herself to the Heart of Christ. In fact, it is precisely this drawing close to Christ in the mystery of His Heart which enables us to dwell on this point - a point in a sense central and also most accessible on the human level - of the revelation of the merciful love of the Father, a revelation which constituted the central content of the messianic mission of the Son of Man.

The Church lives an authentic life when she professes and proclaims mercy - the most stupendous attribute of the Creator and of the Redeemer - and when she brings people close to the sources of the Saviour's mercy, of which she is

58

the trustee and dispenser. Of great significance in this area is constant meditation on the Word of God, and above all conscious and mature participation in the Eucharist and in the sacrament of Penance or Reconciliation. The Eucharist brings us ever nearer to that love which is more powerful than death: "For as often as we eat this bread and drink this cup," we proclaim not only the death of the Redeemer but also His resurrection, "until he comes" in glory.[114] The same Eucharistic rite, celebrated in memory of Him who in His messianic mission revealed the Father to us by means of His words and His cross, attests to the inexhaustible love by virtue of which He desires always to be united with us and present in our midst, coming to meet every human heart. It is the sacrament of Penance or Reconciliation that prepares the way for each individual, even those weighed down with great faults. In this sacrament each person can experience mercy in a unique way, that is, the love which is more powerful than sin. This has already been spoken of in the encyclical *Redemptor hominis*; but it will be fitting to return once more to this fundamental theme.

It is precisely because sin exists in the world, which "God so loved…that he gave his only Son,"[115] that God, who "is love,"[116] cannot reveal Himself otherwise than as mercy. This corresponds not only to the most profound truth of that love which God is, but also to the whole interior truth of man and of the world which is man's temporary homeland.

Mercy in itself, as a perfection of the infinite God, is also infinite. Also infinite therefore and inexhaustible is the Father's readiness to receive the prodigal children who return to His home. Infinite are the readiness and power of forgiveness which flow continually from the marvellous value of the sacrifice of the Son. No human sin can prevail over this power or even limit it. On the part of man only a lack of good will can limit it, a lack of readiness to be converted and to repent, in other words persistence in obstinacy, opposing grace and truth, especially in the face of the witness of the cross and resurrection of Christ.

Therefore, the Church professes and proclaims conversion. Conversion to God always consists in discovering His mercy, that is, in discovering that love which is patient and kind[117] as only the Creator and Father can be; the love to which the "God and Father of our Lord Jesus Christ"[118] is faithful to the uttermost consequences in the history of His covenant with man; even to the cross and to the death and resurrection of the Son. Conversion to God is always the fruit of the rediscovery of this Father, who is rich in mercy.

Authentic knowledge of the God of mercy, the God of tender love, is a constant and inexhaustible source of conversion, not only as a momentary interior act but also as a permanent attitude, as a state of mind. Those who come to know God in this way, who "see" Him in this way, can live only in a state of being continually converted to Him. They live, therefore, in *statu conversionis*; and it is this state of conversion which marks out the most profound element of the pilgrimage of every man and woman on earth in *statu viatoris*. It is obvious that the Church professes the mercy of God, revealed in the crucified and risen Christ, not only by the word of her teaching but above all through the deepest pulsation of the life of the whole People of God. By means of this testimony of life, the Church fulfills the mission proper to the People of God, the mission which is a sharing in and, in a sense, a continuation of the messianic mission of Christ Himself.

The contemporary Church is profoundly conscious that only on the basis of the mercy of God will she be able to carry out the tasks that derive from the teaching of the Second Vatican Council, and, in the first place, the ecumenical task which aims at uniting all those who confess Christ. As she makes many efforts in this direction, the Church confesses with humility that only that love which is more powerful than the weakness of human divisions can definitively bring about that unity which Christ implored from the Father and which the Spirit never ceases to beseech for us "with sighs too deep for words."[119]

### The Church seeks to put mercy into practice

Jesus Christ taught that man not only receives and experiences the mercy of God, but that he is also called "to practise mercy" towards others: "Blessed are the merciful, for they shall obtain mercy."[120] The Church sees in these words a call to action, and she tries to practise mercy. All the beatitudes of the Sermon on the Mount indicate the way of conversion and of reform of life, but the one referring to those who are merciful is particularly eloquent in this regard. Man attains to the merciful love of God, His mercy, to the extent that he himself is interiorly transformed in the spirit of that love towards his neighbour.

This authentically evangelical process is not just a spiritual transformation realised once and for all: it is a whole lifestyle, an essential and continuous characteristic of the Christian vocation. It consists in the constant discovery and persevering practice of love as a unifying and also elevating power despite all difficulties of a psychological or social nature: it is a question, in fact, of a merciful love which, by its essence, is a creative love. In reciprocal relationships between persons merciful love is never a unilateral act or process. Even in the cases in which everything would seem to indicate that only one party is giving and offering, and the other only receiving and taking (for example, in the case of a physician giving treatment, a teacher teaching, parents supporting and bringing up their children, a benefactor helping the needy), in reality the one who gives is always also a beneficiary. In any case, he too can easily find himself in the position of the one who receives, who obtains a benefit, who experiences merciful love; he too can find himself the object of mercy.

In this sense Christ crucified is for us the loftiest model, inspiration and encouragement. When we base ourselves on this disquieting model, we are able with all humility to show mercy to others, knowing that Christ accepts it as if it were shown to Himself.[121] On the basis of this model, we must also continually purify all our actions and all our intentions in which mercy is understood and practised in a unilateral way, as a good done to others. An act of merciful love is only really such when we are deeply convinced at the moment that we perform it that we are at the same time receiving mercy from the people who are accepting it from us. If this bilateral and reciprocal quality is absent, our actions are not yet true acts of mercy, nor has there yet been fully completed in us that conversion to which Christ has shown us the way by His words and example, even to the cross, nor are we yet sharing fully in the magnificent source of merciful love that has been revealed to us by Him.

Thus, the way which Christ showed to us in the Sermon on the Mount with the beatitude regarding those who are merciful is much richer than what we sometimes find in ordinary human opinions about mercy. These opinions see mercy as a unilateral act or process, presupposing and maintaining a certain distance between the one practicing mercy and the one benefitting from it, between the one who does good and the one who receives it. Hence the attempt to free interpersonal and social relationships from mercy and to base them solely on justice. However, such opinions about mercy fail to see the fundamental link between mercy and justice spoken of by the whole biblical tradition, and above all by the messianic mission of Jesus Christ. True mercy is, so to speak, the most profound source of justice. If justice is in itself suitable for "arbitration" between people concerning the reciprocal distribution of objective goods in an equitable manner, love and only love (including that kindly love that we call "mercy") is capable of restoring man to Himself.

Mercy that is truly Christian is also, in a certain sense, the most perfect incarnation of "equality" between people, and therefore also the most perfect incarnation of justice as well, insofar as justice aims at the same result in its own sphere. However, the equality brought by justice is limited to the realm of objective and extrinsic goods, while love and mercy bring it about that people meet one another in that value which is man himself, with the dignity that is proper to him. At the same time, "equality" of people through "patient and kind" love[122] does not take away differences: the person who gives becomes more generous when he feels at the same time benefitted by the person accepting his gift; and vice versa, the person who accepts the gift with the awareness that, in accepting it, he too is doing good is in his own way serving the great cause of the dignity of the person; and this contributes to uniting people in a more profound manner.

Thus, mercy becomes an indispensable element for shaping mutual relationships between people, in a spirit of deepest respect for what is human, and in a spirit of mutual brotherhood. It is impossible to establish this bond between people, if they wish to regulate their mutual relationships solely according to the measure of justice. In every sphere of interpersonal relationships justice must, so to speak, be "corrected " to a considerable extent by that love which, as St Paul proclaims, "is patient and kind" or, in other words, possesses the characteristics of that merciful love which is so much of the essence of the Gospel and Christianity. Let us remember, furthermore, that merciful love also means the cordial tenderness and sensitivity so eloquently spoken of in the parable of the prodigal son,[123] and also in the parables of the lost sheep and the lost coin.[124] Consequently, merciful love is supremely indispensable between those who are closest to one another: between husbands and wives, between parents and children, between friends; and it is indispensable in education and in pastoral work.

Its sphere of action, however, is not limited to this. If Paul VI more than once indicated the civilisation of love[125] as the goal towards which all efforts in the cultural and social fields as well as in the economic and political fields should tend. It must be added that this good will never be reached if in our thinking and acting concerning the vast and complex spheres of human society we stop at the criterion of "an eye for an eye, a tooth for a tooth"[126] and do not try to transform it in its essence, by complementing it with another spirit. Certainly, the Second Vatican Council also leads us in this direction, when it speaks repeatedly of the need to make the world more human,[127] and says that the realisation of this task is precisely the mission of the Church in the modern world. Society can become ever more human only if we introduce into the many-sided setting of interpersonal and social relationships, not merely justice, but also that "merciful love" which constitutes the messianic message of the Gospel.

Society can become "ever more human" only when we introduce into all the mutual relationships which form its moral aspect the moment of forgiveness, which is so much of the essence of the Gospel. Forgiveness demonstrates the presence in the world of the love which is more powerful than sin. Forgiveness is also the fundamental condition for reconciliation, not only in the relationship of God with man, but also in relationships between people. A world from which forgiveness was eliminated would be nothing but a world of cold and unfeeling justice, in the name of which each person would claim his or her own rights vis-a-vis others; the various kinds of selfishness latent in man would transform life and human society into a system of oppression of the weak by the strong, or into an arena of permanent strife between one group and another.

For this reason, the Church must consider it one of her principal duties - at every stage of history and especially in our modern age - to proclaim and to introduce into life the mystery of mercy, supremely revealed in Jesus Christ. Not only for the Church herself as the community of believers but also in a certain sense for all humanity, this mystery is the source of a life different from the life which can be built by man, who is exposed to the oppressive forces of the threefold concupiscence active within him.[128] It is precisely in the name of this mystery that Christ teaches us to forgive always. How often we repeat the words of the prayer which He Himself taught us, asking "forgive us our trespasses as we forgive those who trespass against us," which means those who are guilty of something in our regard[129] It is indeed difficult to express the profound value of the attitude which these words describe and inculcate. How many things these words say to every individual about others and also about himself. The consciousness of being trespassers against each other goes hand in hand with the call to fraternal solidarity, which St Paul expressed in his concise exhortation to "forbear one another in love."[130] What a lesson of humility is to be found here with regard to man, with regard both to one's neighbour and to oneself What a school of good will for daily living, in the various conditions of our existence. If we were to ignore this lesson, what would remain of any "humanist" program of life and education?

Christ emphasises so insistently the need to forgive others that when Peter asked Him how many times he should forgive his neighbour He answered with the symbolic number of "seventy times seven,"[131] meaning that he must be able to forgive everyone every time. It is obvious that such a generous requirement of forgiveness does not cancel out the objective requirements of justice. Properly understood, justice constitutes, so to speak, the goal of forgiveness. In no passage of the Gospel message does forgiveness, or mercy as its source, mean indulgence towards evil, towards scandals, towards injury or insult. In any case, reparation for evil and scandal, compensation for injury, and satisfaction for insult are conditions for forgiveness.

Thus the fundamental structure of justice always enters into the sphere of mercy. Mercy, however, has the power to confer on justice a new content, which is expressed most simply and fully in forgiveness. Forgiveness, in fact, shows that, over and above the process of "compensation" and "truce" which is specific to justice, love is necessary, so that man may affirm himself as man. Fulfillment of the conditions of justice is especially indispensable in order that love may reveal its own nature. In analysing the parable of the prodigal son, we have already called attention to the fact that he who forgives and he who is forgiven encounter one another at an essential point, namely the dignity or essential value of the person, a point which cannot be lost and the affirmation of which, or its rediscovery, is a source of the greatest joy.[132]

The Church rightly considers it her duty and the purpose of her mission to guard the authenticity of forgiveness, both in life and behaviour and in educational and pastoral work. She protects it simply by guarding its source, which is the mystery of the mercy of God Himself as revealed in Jesus Christ.

The basis of the Church's mission, in all the spheres spoken of in the numerous pronouncements of the most recent Council and in the centuries-old experience of the apostolate, is none other than "drawing from the wells of the Saviour"[133] this is what provides many guidelines for the mission of the Church in the lives of individual Christians, of individual communities, and also of the whole People of God. This "drawing from the wells of the Saviour" can be done only in the spirit of that poverty to which we are called by the words and example of the Lord: "You received without pay, give without pay."[134] Thus, in all the ways of the Church's life and ministry - through the evangelical poverty of her ministers and stewards and of the whole people which bears witness to "the mighty works" of its Lord - the God who is "rich in mercy" has been made still more clearly manifest.

# The Prayer of the Church in Our Times

## The Church appeals to the mercy of God

The Church proclaims the truth of God's mercy revealed in the crucified and risen Christ, and she professes it in various ways. Furthermore, she seeks to practise mercy towards people through people, and she sees in this an indispensable condition for solicitude for a better and "more human" world, today and tomorrow. However, at no time and in no historical period - especially at a moment as critical as our own - can the Church forget the prayer that is a cry for the mercy of God amid the many forms of evil which weigh upon humanity and threaten it. Precisely this is the fundamental right and duty of the Church in Christ Jesus, her right and duty towards God and towards humanity. The more the human conscience succumbs to secularisation, loses its sense of the very meaning of the word "mercy," moves away from God and distances itself from the mystery of mercy, the more the Church has the right and the duty to appeal to the God of mercy "with loud cries."[135] These "loud cries" should be the mark of the Church of our times, cries uttered to God to implore His mercy, the certain manifestation of which she professes and proclaims as having already come in Jesus crucified and risen, that is, in the Paschal Mystery. It is this mystery which bears within itself the most complete revelation of mercy, that is, of that love which is more powerful than death, more powerful than sin and every evil, the love which lifts man up when he falls into the abyss and frees him from the greatest threats.

Modern man feels these threats. What has been said above in this regard is only a rough outline. Modern man often anxiously wonders about the solution to the terrible tensions which have built up in the world and which entangle humanity. And if at times he lacks the courage to utter the word "mercy," or if in his conscience empty of religious content he does not find the equivalent, so much greater is the need for the Church to utter his word, not only in her own name but also in the name of all the men and women of our time.

Everything that I have said in the present document on mercy should therefore be continually transformed into an ardent prayer: into a cry that implores mercy according to the needs of man in the modern world. May this cry be full of that truth about mercy which has found such rich expression in Sacred Scripture and in Tradition, as also in the authentic life of faith of countless generations of the People of God. With this cry let us, like the sacred writers, call upon the God who cannot despise anything that He has made,[136] the God who is faithful to Himself, to His fatherhood and His love. And, like the prophets, let us appeal to that love which has maternal characteristics and which, like a mother, follows each of her children, each lost sheep, even if they should number millions, even if in the world evil should prevail over goodness, even if contemporary humanity should deserve a new "flood" on account of its sins, as once the generation of Noah did. Let us have recourse to that fatherly love revealed to us by Christ in His messianic mission, a love which reached its culmination in His cross, in His death and resurrection. Let us have recourse to God through Christ, mindful of the words of Mary's Magnificat, which proclaim mercy "from generation to generation." Let us implore God's mercy for the present generation. May the Church which, following the example of Mary, also seeks to be the spiritual mother of mankind, express in this prayer her maternal solicitude and at the same time her confident love, that love from which is born the most burning need for prayer.

Let us offer up our petitions, directed by the faith, by the hope, and by the charity which Christ has planted in our hearts. This attitude is likewise love of God, whom modern man has sometimes separated far from himself, made extraneous to himself, proclaiming in various ways that God is "superfluous." This is, therefore, love of God, the insulting rejection of whom by modern man we feel profoundly, and we are ready to cry out with Christ on the cross: "Father, forgive them; for they know not what they do."[137] At the same time it is love of people, of all men and women without any exception or division: without difference of race, culture, language, or world outlook, without distinction between friends and enemies. This is love for people - it desires every true good for each individual and for every human community, every family, every nation, every social group, for young people, adults, parents, the elderly - a love for everyone, without exception. This is love, or rather an anxious solicitude to ensure for each individual every true good and to remove and drive away every sort of evil.

And, if any of our contemporaries do not share the faith and hope which lead me, as a servant of Christ and steward of the mysteries of God,[138] to implore God's mercy for humanity in this hour of history, let them at least try to understand the reason for my concern. It is dictated by love for man, for all that is human and which, according to the intuitions of many of our contemporaries, is threatened by an immense danger. The mystery of Christ, which reveals to us the great vocation of man and which led me to emphasise in the encyclical *Redemptor hominis* his incomparable dignity, also obliges me to proclaim mercy as God's merciful love, revealed in that same mystery of Christ. It likewise obliges me to have recourse to that mercy and to beg for it at this difficult, critical phase of the history of the Church and of the world, as we approach the end of the second millennium.

In the name of Jesus Christ crucified and risen, in the spirit of His messianic mission, enduring in the history of humanity, we raise our voices and pray that the Love which is in the Father may once again be revealed at this stage of history, and that, through the work of the Son and Holy Spirit, it may be shown to be present in our modern world and to be more powerful than evil: more powerful than sin and death. We pray for this through the intercession of her who does not cease to proclaim "mercy…from generation to generation," and also through the intercession of those for whom there have been completely fulfilled the words of the Sermon on the Mount: "Blessed are the merciful, for they shall obtain mercy."[139]

In continuing the great task of implementing the Second Vatican Council, in which we can rightly see a new phase of the self- realisation of the Church - in keeping with the epoch in which it has been our destiny to live - the Church herself must be constantly guided by the full consciousness that in this work it is not permissible for her, for any reason, to withdraw into herself. The reason for her existence is, in fact, to reveal God, that Father who allows us to "see" Him in Christ.[140] No matter how strong the resistance of human history may be, no matter how marked the diversity of contemporary civilisation, no matter how great the denial of God in the human world, so much the greater must be the Church's closeness to that mystery which, hidden for centuries in God, was then truly shared with man, in time, through Jesus Christ.

With my apostolic blessing.

*Given in Rome, at St Peter's, on the thirtieth day of November, the First Sunday of Advent, in the year 1980, the third of my pontificate.*

*Joannes Paulus II*

JOHN PAUL II

# Endnotes

[1] *Eph* 2:4.

[2] Cf. *Jn* 1:18; *Heb* 1:1f.

[3] *Jn* 14:8-9.

[4] *Eph* 2:4-5.

[5] 2 *Cor* 1:3.

[6] Pastoral Constitution on the Church in the Modern World *Gaudium et spes*, no. 22: AAS 58 (1966), p. 1042.

[7] Cf. *ibid.*

[8] 1 *Tm* 6:16.

[9] *Rom* 1:20.

[10] *Jn* 1:18.

[11] 1 *Tm* 6:16.

[12] *Ti* 3:4.

[13] *Eph* 2:4.

[14] Cf. *Gn* 1:28.

[15] Pastoral Constitution on the Church in the Modern World *Gaudium et spes*, no. 9: AAS 58 (1966), p. 1032.

[16] 2 *Cor* 1:3.

[17] *Mt* 6:4, 6, 18.

[18] Cf. *Eph* 3:18; also *Lk* 11:5-13.

[19] *Lk* 4:18-19.

[20] *Lk* 7:19.

[21] *Lk* 7:22-23.

[22] 1 *Jn* 4:16.

[23] *Eph* 2:4.

[24] *Lk* 15:11-32.

[25] *Lk* 10:30-37.

[26] *Mt* 18:23-35.

[27] *Mt* 18:12-14; *Lk* 15:3-7.

[28] *Lk* 15:8-10.

[29] *Mt* 22:38.

[30] *Mt* 5:7.

[31] Cf. *Jgs* 3:7-9.

[32] Cf. 1 *Kgs* 8:22-53.

[33] Cf. *Mi* 7:18-20.

[34] Cf. *Is* 1:18; 51:4-16.

[35] Cf. *Bar* 2:11-3, 8.

[36] Cf. *Neh* 9.

[37] Cf. e.g. *Hos* 2:21-25 and 15; *Is* 54:6-8.

[38] Cf. *Jer* 31:20; *Lz* 39:25-29.

[39] Cf. 2 *Sm* 11; 12; 24:10.

[40] *Job passim.*

[41] Est.. 4:17k ff.

[42] Cf. e.g. *Neh* 9:30-32; *Tb* 3:2-3, 11-12; 8:16-17; 1 *Mc* 4:24.

[43] Cf. *Ex* 3:7f.

[44] Cf. *Is* 63:9.

[45] *Ex* 34:6.

[46] Cf. *Nm* 14:18; 2 *Chr* 30:9; *Neh* 9:17; *Ps* 86(85); *Wis* 15:1; *Sir* 2:11; *Jl* 2:13.

[47] Cf. *Is* 63:16.

[48] Cf. *Ex* 4:22.

[49] Cf. *Hos* 2:3.

[50] Cf. *Hos* 11:7-9; *Jer* 31:20; *Is* 54:7f.

[51] Cf. *Ps* 103(102) and 145(144).

[52] In describing mercy, the books of the Old Testament use two expressions in particular, each having a different semantic nuance. First there is the term *hesed*, which indicates a profound attitude of "goodness." When this is established between two individuals, they do not just wish each other well; they are also faithful to each other by virtue of an interior commitment, and therefore also by virtue of a faithfulness to themselves. Since *hesed* also means "grace" or "love," this occurs precisely on the basis of this fidelity. The fact that the commitment in question has not only a moral character but almost a juridical one makes no difference. When in the Old Testament the word *hesed* is used of the Lord, this always occurs in connection with the covenant that God established with Israel. This covenant was, on God's part, a gift and a grace for Israel. Nevertheless, since, in harmony with the covenant entered into, God had made a commitment to respect it, *hesed* also acquired in a certain sense a legal content. The juridical commitment on God's part ceased to oblige whenever Israel broke the covenant and did not respect its conditions. But precisely at this point, *hesed*, in ceasing to be a juridical obligation, revealed its deeper aspect: it showed itself as what it was at the beginning, that is, as love that gives, love more powerful than betrayal, grace stronger than sin.

This fidelity vis-a-vis the unfaithful "daughter of my people" (cf. *Lam* 4:3, 6) is, in brief, on God's part, fidelity to Himself. This becomes obvious in the frequent recurrence together of the two terms *hesed* we've met (= grace and fidelity), which could be considered a case of *hendiadys* (cf. e.g. *Ex* 34:6; 2 *Sm* 2:6; 15:20; *Ps* 25[24]:10; 40[39]:11-12; 85[84]:11; 138[137]:2; *Mi* 7:20). "It is not for your sake, O house of Israel, that I am about to act, but for the sake of my holy name" (*Ez* 36:22). Therefore Israel, although burdened with guilt for having broken the covenant, cannot lay claim to God's hesed on the basis of (legal) justice; yet it can and must go on hoping and trusting to obtain it, since the God of the covenant is really "responsible for his love." The fruits of this love are forgiveness and restoration to grace, the reestablishment of the interior covenant.

The second word which in the terminology of the Old Testament serves to define mercy is *rahamim*. This has a different nuance from that of *hesed*. While *hesed* highlights the marks of fidelity to self and of "responsibility for one's own love" (which are in a certain sense masculine characteristics), *rahamim*, in its very root, denotes the love of a mother (*rehem* = mother's womb). From the deep and original bond - indeed the unity - that links a mother to her child there springs a particular relationship to the child, a particular love. Of this love one can say that it is completely gratuitous, not merited, and that in this aspect it constitutes an interior necessity: an exigency of the heart. It is, as it were, a "feminine" variation of the masculine fidelity to self expressed by *hesed*. Against this psychological background, *rahamim* generates a whole range of feelings, including goodness and tenderness, patience and understanding, that is, readiness to forgive.

The Old Testament attributes to the Lord precisely these characteristics when it uses the term *rahamim* in speaking of Him. We read in Isaiah: "Can a woman forget her suckling child, that she should have no compassion on the son of her womb? Even these may forget, yet I will not forget you" (*Is* 49:15). This love, faithful and invincible thanks to the mysterious power of motherhood, is expressed in the Old Testament texts in various ways: as salvation from dangers, especially from enemies; also as forgiveness of sins - of individuals and also of the whole of Israel; and finally in readiness to fulfill the (eschatological) promise and hope, in spite of human infidelity, as we read in Hosea: "I will heal their faithlessness, I will love them freely" (*Hos* 14:5).

In the terminology of the Old Testament we also find other expressions, referring in different ways to the same basic content. But the two terms mentioned above deserve special attention. They clearly show their original anthropomorphic aspect: in describing God's mercy, the biblical authors use terms that correspond to the consciousness and experience of their contemporaries. The Greek terminology in the Septuagint translation does not show as great a wealth as the Hebrew: therefore it does not offer all the semantic nuances proper to the original text. At any rate, the New Testament builds upon the wealth and depth that already marked the Old.

In this way, we have inherited from the Old Testament - as it were in a special synthesis - not only the wealth of expressions used by those books in order to define God's mercy, but also a specific and obviously anthropomorphic "psychology" of God: the image of His anxious love, which in contact with evil, and in particular with the sin of the individual and of the people, is manifested as mercy. This image is made up not only of the rather general content of the verb *hanan* but also of the content of hesed and *rahamim*. The term *hanan* expresses a wider concept: it means in fact the manifestation of grace, which involves, so to speak, a constant predisposition to be generous, benevolent and merciful. In addition to these basic semantic elements, the Old Testament concept of mercy is also made up of what is included in the verb *hamal*, which literally means "to spare" (a defeated enemy) but also "to show mercy and compassion," and in consequence forgiveness and remission of guilt. There is also the term *hus*, which expresses pity and compassion, but especially in the affective sense. These terms appear more rarely in the biblical texts to denote mercy. In addition, one must note the word '*emet*' already mentioned: it means primarily "solidity, security" (in the Greek of the Septuagint: "truth") and then "fidelity," land in this way it seems to link up with the semantic content proper to the term *hesed*.

[53] *Ps* 40(39):11; 98(97):2f.;
*Is* 45:21; 51:5, 8; 56:1.

[54] *Wis* 11:24.

[55] 1 *Jn* 4:16.

[56] *Jer* 31:3.

[57] *Is* 54:10.

[58] *Jon* 4:2, 11; *Ps* 145(144):9; *Sir* 18:8-14; *Wis* 11:23-12:1.

[59] *Jn* 14:9.

[60] In both places it is a case of hesed, i..e., the fidelity that God manifests to His own love for the people, fidelity to the promises that will find their definitive fulfillment precisely in the motherhood of the Mother of God (cf. *Lk* 1:49-54).

[61] Cf. *Lk* 1:72. Here too it is a case of mercy in the meaning of hesed, insofar as in the following sentences, in which Zechariah speaks of the "tender mercy of our God," there is clearly expressed the second meaning, namely, rahamim (Latin translation: *viscera misericordiae*), which rather identifies God's mercy with a mother's love.

[62] Cf. *Lk* 15:14-32.

[63] *Lk* 15:18-19.

[64] *Lk* 15:20.

[65] *Lk* 15:32.

[66] Cf. *Lk* 15:3-6.
[67] Cf. *Lk* 15:8-9.
[68] 1 *Cor* 13:4-8.
[69] Cf. *Rom* 12:21.
[70] Cf. the liturgy of the Easter Vigil: the Exsultet.
[71] *Acts* 10:38.
[72] *Mt* 9:35.
[73] Cf. *Mk* 15:37; *Jn* 19:30.
[74] *Is* 53:5
[75] 2 *Cor* 5:21.
[76] *Ibid.*
[77] The Nicene-Constantinopolitan Creed.
[78] *Jn* 3:16.
[79] Cf. *Jn* 14:9.
[80] *Mt* 10:28.
[81] *Phil* 2:8.
[82] 2 *Cor* 5:21.
[83] Cf. 1 *Cor* 15:54-55.
[84] Cf. *Lk* 4:18-21.
[85] Cf. *Lk* 7:20-23.
[86] Cf. *Is* 35:5; 61:1-3.
[87] 1 *Cor* 15:4.
[88] *Rv* 21:1.
[89] *Rv* 21:4.
[90] Cf. *Rv* 21:4.
[91] *Rv* 3:20.
[92] Cf. *Mt* 24:35.
[93] Cf. *Rv* 3:20.
[94] *Mt* 25:40.
[95] *Mt* 5:7.
[96] *Jn* 14:9.
[97] *Rom* 8:32.
[98] *Mk* 12:27.
[99] *Jn* 20:19-23.
[100] *Ps* 89(88):2.
[101] *Lk* 1:50.
[102] Cf. 2 *Cor* 1:21-22.
[103] *Lk* 1:50.
[104] Cf. *Ps* 85(84):11.
[105] *Lk* 1:50.
[106] Cf. *Lk* 4:18.
[107] Cf. *Lk* 7:22.
[108] Dogmatic Constitution on the Church *Lumen gentium*, no. 62: AAS 57 1965), p. 63.
[109] Pastoral Constitution on the Church in the Modern World *Gaudium et spes*, no. 10: AAS 58 (1966), p. 1032.
[110] *Ibid.*
[111] *Mt* 5:38.
[112] Cf. *Jn* 14:9-10.
[113] *Jn* 14:9.
[114] Cf. 1 *Cor* 11:26; acclamation in the Roman Missal.
[115] *Jn* 3:16.
[116] 1 *Jn* 4:8.
[117] Cf. 1 *Cor* 13:4.
[118] 2 *Cor* 1:3.
[119] *Rom* 8:26.
[120] *Mt* 5:7.
[121] Cf. *Mt* 25:34-40.
[122] Cf. 1 *Cor* 13:4.
[123] Cf. *Lk* 15:11-32.

80

[124] Cf. *Lk* 15:1-10.
[125] Cf. *Insegnamenti di Paolo VI*, XIII (1975), p. 1568 (close of the Holy Year, December 25, 1975).
[126] *Mt* 5:38.
[127] Cf. Pastoral Constitution on the Church in the Modern World *Gaudium et spes*, no. 40 AAS 58 (1966), pp. 1057-1059; Pope Paul VI: Apostolic Exhortation *Paterna cum benevolentia*, in particular nos. 1-6: AAS 67 (1975), pp. 7-9, 17-23.
[128] Cf. 1 *Jn* 2:16.
[129] *Mt* 6:12.
[130] *Eph* 4:2; cf. *Gal* 6:2.
[131] *Mt* 18:22.
[132] Cf. *Lk* 15:32.
[133] Cf. *Is* 12:3.
[134] *Mt* 10:8.
[136] Cf. *Wis* 11:24; *Ps* 145(144):9; *Gn* 1:31.
[137] *Lk* 23:34.
[138] Cf. 1 *Cor* 4:1.
[139] *Mt* 5:7.
[140] Cf. *Jn* 14:9.

**Images:** Page 14: The Return of the Prodigal Son, 1654-55 (oil on canvas), Guercino (Giovanni Francesco Barbieri) (1591-1666) / The Putnam Foundation, Timken Museum of Art, San Diego, USA / Bridgeman. Page 30: MS 49 f.7 Christ Crucified by the Virtues, illustration from the Regensburg Lectionary, c.1267-76 (vellum), German School, (13th century) / Keble College, Oxford, UK / By Kind Permission of the Warden and Fellows of Keble College, Oxford / Bridgeman Images.